Oxford University Press, Great Clarendon Street, Oxford OX2 6DP

Oxford   New York
Athens Auckland Bangkok Bogotá
Buenos Aires Calcutta Cape Town Chennai
Dar es Salaam Delhi Florence Hong Kong Istanbul
Karachi Kuala Lumpur Madrid Melbourne
Mexico City Mumbai Nairobi Paris São Paulo Singapore
Taipei Tokyo Toronto Warsaw

and associated companies in
Berlin Ibadan

Oxford is a trade mark of Oxford University Press

© Oxford University Press 1995
5 7 9 10 8 6

First published 1995

A CIP catalogue record for this book is available from the British Library

ISBN 0-19-910332-1 (hardback)
ISBN 0-19-910364-X (paperback)

Printed in Hong Kong

My first alphabet book

Illustrated by Julie Park

OXFORD

UNIVERSITY PRESS

my name is

_____

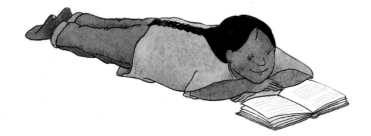

Aa

abcdefghijklmnopqrstuvwxyz

alphabet   ambulance

animals   ants   apple   arrow

Bb

ball balloon banana bear

bed book bus

Cc

cake   candle   car   cat

caterpillar   computer   cup

Dd

dinosaur   dog   doll   donkey

door   duck

Ee

egg   elephant   envelope

Ff

feather   fire   fish   foot

fork   fox

Gg

game   garage   garden
gate   ghost   goat

Hh

hair hand hat head

hill house

Ii

ink   insects   instruments

invitation

jack-in-the-box   jam   jar

jigsaw   jug

Kk

**kangaroo kettle key
kite kitten**

ladder   lamb   lead   leaf
lion   log

Mm

magnet   map   monkey

moon   mushroom

Nn

nail   necklace   nest   night

number   nut

Oo

octopus   orange   ostrich

Pp

paint　paper　pencil

picture　puppet　puppy

Qq

queen question

Rr

rabbit   rainbow   rat

rhinoceros   rocket   rose

Ss

sand   sandwich   sea   seal

sock   sun

Tt

table teddy bear tail

telephone television tiger

umbrella   under

Vv

van   vegetable   video

volcano

wall   wasp   watch   whale

whistle   wool

Xx

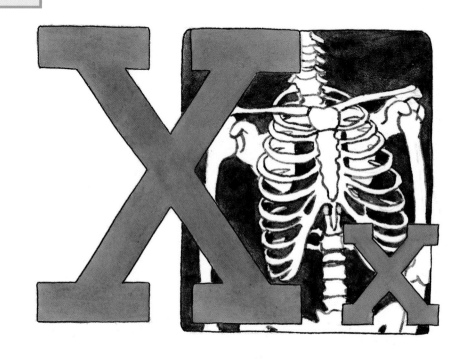

X-ray

Yy

yacht yo-yo

Zz

zebra zigzag

Here are more surprises hidden in the pictures. Can you find them?

anchor	guitar	paintbrush	toothpaste
		person	top
bee	helicopter	pillow	towel
bird		pink	toys
bottle	jelly	pyjamas	
butterfly			water
button	king	red	white
		ring	
camera	ladybird	rope	yellow
card	leg	ruler	
castle			
	mirror	saucer	
dictionary	money	seaweed	
	mouse	sea-horse	
	mouth		
eggshell	mug		
face			
fairy	nine		
fence			
footprint